SMART GIRLS

DIARIES AND KEEPSAKES

Style Secrets for Girls

STEPHANIE TURNBULL

W
FRANKLIN WATTS
LONDON • SYDNEY

An Appleseed Editions book

First published in 2014 by Franklin Watts
338 Euston Road, London NW1 3BH

Franklin Watts Australia
Hachette Children's Books
Level 17/207 Kent St, Sydney, NSW 2000

© 2013 Appleseed Editions

Created by Appleseed Editions Ltd,
Well House, Friars Hill, Guestling,
East Sussex TN35 4ET

Designed and illustrated by Guy Callaby
Edited by Mary-Jane Wilkins

ISBN 978-1-4451-3183-2

Dewey Classification: 745.5'938

A CIP catalogue for this book is available from the British Library.

Picture credits
t = top, b = bottom, l = left, r = right, c = centre
title page Christopher Halloran/Shutterstock; 2t Aleksandr Bryliaev, b artzenter/both Shutterstock; 3t Studio DMM Photography,
Designs & Art, inset kostudio/both Shutterstock; 4 Ilike, b Africa Studio/both Shutterstock; 5t badge James Clarke, teddy Milos
Luzanin, flag Annmarie Young, postcards bepsy, snowglobe MarFot/all Shutterstock, medal Guy Callaby, l Hemera/Thinkstock,
stamp catwalker/Shutterstock.com, b Stephen Chung/Shutterstock; 6 diaries: heart-shaped sagir, blue Gabriel Nardelli Araujo, red
spillikin, leather pio3, hands holding book Tatiana Popova, diary with post-its schab/Shutterstock, b nuttakit/all Shutterstock;
7t ueapun, r Adrian Hughes, b folders Hong Vo, punch and cards ben44, tags Paul Gibbings, ribbon WitthayaP, paperclips Elena
Blokhina/all Shutterstock; 8tr Jo Ann Snover, t Rob Hyrons/both Shutterstock; 10tl Begum Ozpinar, r & c Raymond Kasprzak, teapot
bookmark Cousin_Avi, open diary Pedro Nogueira, bl sagir, br Nata-Lia/all Shutterstock; 11 Victoria Brassey/Shutterstock;
12 doodles JeremyWhat, stars ildogesto, faces Murat emir colcu, b Cheryl Casey/all Shutterstock; 13c holbox, l Kiselev Andrey
Valerevich, cr mojito.mak[dog]gmail.com, notepaper happydancing/all Shutterstock, r Neftali/Shutterstock.com; 14t
lkphotographers, r Ints Vikmanis, b Baronb/all Shutterstock; 15t Lamella/Shutterstock, c iStockphoto/Thinkstock, r & b vovan, pen
jedka84/all Shutterstock; 16t DNF Style, tent Serg Zastavkin, girls and camera irina.roibu, girl with hat cabania, three girls dotshock,
girls on beach oliveromg, l Andi Berger/all Shutterstock; 17t Anatoliy Samara, sunflower frame Santiago Cornejo, photo inside Samuel
Borges Photography, roses frame Dmitri Mikitenko, dog JulijaSapic_Portfolio, bead frame Dr Ajay Kumar Singh, hijab girl Zurijeta,
orange frame Brooke Becker, tug-of-war oliveromg/all Shutterstock, b iStockphoto/Thinkstock; 18 waiter iStockphoto/Thinkstock,
stamp Neftali/Shutterstock.com, metro sign iStockphoto/Thinkstock, sign Julian de Dios/all Shutterstock, Eiffel Tower iStockphoto/
Thinkstock, ticket AKaiser/Shutterstock, old stamp Halima Ahkdar/Shutterstock.com, cl jan kranendonk, c aldorado/both
Shutterstock, b waiter, Rue de Croissant, Eiffel Tower from boat/all iStockphoto/Thinkstock, bow trekandshoot, envelope alien-tz/
both Shutterstock; 19 br hole punch Bara22, scissors tetyana radchenko, bl Alexandr Makarov/all Shutterstock; 20t kuleczka,
l crazycolors, b Hannamariah/both Shutterstock; 21 sledge girl Smailhodzic, r Snaprender/all Shutterstock; 22 pegs and line Jag_cz, girl
and dog Nuzza, Muslim girl ansar80, girls on bench Olesia Bilkei, b girl winking Timofeeva
Maria, frames Archipoch/Shutterstock; 24t Catherine Murray, l Fuse/both Shutterstock;
r & b iStockphoto/Thinkstock; 25b Ysbrand Cosijn/Shutterstock; 26tr boomerang Ashwin,
coathanger R. Gino Santa Maria, coloured pencils Jordi Muray, pot Tramont_ana/all
Shutterstock, b iStockphoto/Thinkstock; 27t book ene, ticket Olga Kovalenko, sellotape
Shane White/all Shutterstock, ribbon iStockphoto/Thinkstock, map Brand X Pictures/both
Thinkstock; 28 MANDY GODBEHEAR/Shutterstock; 29r Patrizia Tilly, b Hank Frentz/both
Shutterstock; 30b Sharon Day/Shutterstock; 32 Uli Eckardt/Shutterstock
Front cover: OtnaYdur/Shutterstock

Printed in China

Franklin Watts is a division of Hachette Children's Books,
an Hachette UK company.
www.hachette.co.uk

Contents

All about you

Think about all the things that make you unique – your ideas, memories, interests and ambitions. Writing a diary and surrounding yourself with treasured possessions is a great way of expressing yourself. It's fun, too!

Dear diary...

Diaries are perfect for recording important events and experiences, or just having a good rant to get something off your chest! Writing down feelings, fears or worries can make you feel much better – and jotting ideas, lists or plans keeps you organized.

Magical memories

Keepsakes are objects that remind you of special times, people and places. They might be gifts, photos, collections, prizes or well-loved toys. Whether they're priceless **heirlooms** or cheap souvenirs, the point is that they are precious to YOU.

Be selective with your stuff. What's important and what's just junk?

Pssst... Hot Tip!

Look out for these tips throughout the book. They give you all kinds of extra advice and ideas for creating special diaries and displays.

Fun diary facts

One of the earliest diaries was written in the 2nd century by a Roman Emperor called Marcus Aurelius.

DEUTSCHE BUNDESPOST

ANNE FRANK · 12.6.1929 · 31.3.1945

1979

Possibly the most famous **diarist** ever was Anne Frank, a Jewish teenager whose family hid in Amsterdam during the Second World War.

Nowadays, many people compose online diaries, or **blogs**, which can be read by friends – or complete strangers!

Choose your diary

Diaries come in all different shapes and sizes. They may be huge, thick journals with space for detailed descriptions of each day, or slim pocket books for brief notes and quick lists. So which one is right for you?

Diary types

First, think whether you want to write a daily account of your life, or only occasional entries when something really interesting happens. A tiny, dainty diary is no use if you run out of space, while a vast, empty page to fill every day could be daunting!

You can always clip or tape extra pages in your diary.

Pssst... If you're not keen on writing by hand, use a computer, but be sure to back up your work regularly – it would be terrible to lose everything!

Pick and choose

Remember that diaries don't have to cover a whole year – how about keeping a holiday journal, or writing a summary of each week, month or school term? You could also **review** films you've watched, books you've read or places you've visited.

Neat notebooks

It's often better (and cheaper!) to buy a good notebook instead of a diary. This lets you write as much or little as you want, whenever you want. Start each entry on a new page and remember to put the date at the top.

Packs of small notebooks don't cost much and always come in handy.

Make your own

If no diary or notebook is quite right, create your own. Punch holes in paper and tie them together with **treasury tags**, ribbon or wool. You could also write on A4 sheets and file them in a ring binder, or help the environment and recycle scrap paper.

Be creative and use lots of bright, cheerful colours.

Cool covers

A beautiful cover transforms an ordinary book into a special journal that you'll be keen to start writing in! Try one of these clever cover ideas, using colours and designs that reflect your personal style.

Smart jackets

Here's a neat way of making a simple jacket using paper, gift wrap or wallpaper. Swap it for a new one whenever you want!

1. Cut a piece of paper about 5 cm bigger than your open diary at the top and bottom and about 12 cm wider at each end.

5 cm

12 cm

2. Crease the paper at the top and bottom edges of the diary, then move the diary out of the way and fold the paper neatly along the creases.

3. Place the open diary in the centre of the folded paper. Wrap the left end of the paper over the front cover and crease at the edge.

4. Now slide the front cover into the sleeve you've created.

5. *Shut the diary and wrap the other end of the paper over the back cover. Fold in and crease along the edge.*

Don't have the book open, or your finished jacket will be too small.

6. *Slide the back cover into the sleeve.*

7. *If you want, decorate with stickers, pen doodles, or pictures cut from magazines.*

Funky fabric

Make a fashion statement by dressing up your diary! You'll need an old shirt with a top pocket.

Pssst... Kids' shirts are ideal for this as the pockets are small.

1. *Lay the shirt and diary face down, with the pocket in the middle of the cover and the edge of the shirt lined up with the diary edge. Draw around the diary.*

3. *Lay the material in place and tuck in the long, cut edge so it doesn't fray. Keep it in place with **PVA glue** or a few stitches.*

4. *Spread glue over the front cover and stick on the material. Glue the top and bottom edges inside the front cover. Leave to dry, then cover the back in the same way.*

2. *Carefully cut along the three sides about 2 cm outside the lines you drew.*

5. *Use the front pocket as a handy place to store pens!*

Diary decorations

You can decorate your diary with much more than just a cover! Try these ideas for all kinds of imaginative extras to make your diary one of a kind.

Bling it up

Give your diary some glitz by gluing on gems or sequins, and hang key rings or charms from the rings of spiral-bound books. Make a fancy fastener by threading beads on thin elastic, tying it in a loop and stretching it around the diary to keep it firmly shut.

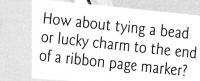
How about tying a bead or lucky charm to the end of a ribbon page marker?

Ribbon markers

Some diaries and notebooks have ribbon page markers attached, but if yours doesn't, tape a ribbon to the inside back cover – or weave one up through the loops of a spiral-bound diary and leave the end to hang inside the book.

Another method is to loop ribbon through a paper clip, then pull the ends through the loop. Attach your clip to a page.

Make several ribbon clips to mark different pages.

Pssst... Stick decorated envelopes inside your diary for storing bits and bobs such as photos or secret notes.

Perfect pens

Once your diary looks fab, you'll want a beautiful pen to go with it! Colourful pipe cleaners are great for livening up plain pens and pencils. Coil them around the end and add extra decorations...

... or fold one in half around strands of wool...

... then thread on a few beads...

...and wrap the pipe cleaner around the top of your pen.

Start scribbling!

So you've got your diary and you're ready to write – now get started! Here are some helpful tips to keep you motivated and make sure you don't give up. Remember, the more you write, the more important your diary will become.

Make time

Diary-writing has to be part of your regular routine if it's to become a habit. Set aside some time each day, perhaps in the evening after homework. If you're too tired by then, how about getting up ten minutes earlier in the morning to write?

Be flexible

A diary isn't schoolwork, it's for YOU – so there are no rules about what to write! If you feel you must include every detail of your day then diary-writing will soon become a chore. Get straight to the important stuff and say how you feel about it.

Don't spend all evening watching TV! Set aside half an hour for diary-writing.

Try using stickers to express how good or bad your day has been.

Mix it up

Your diary can be the place for everything that's going on in your head – ideas, opinions, dreams, poems or wish lists. Jot down inspiring or funny **quotations**, useful recipes or random facts. The more variety you include, the more interesting your diary will be to look back on later.

If you don't feel like writing about real life, why not have some fun and imagine you're a spoilt celebrity, rock star or superhero?

"Tried on dresses for the Oscars. Can't decide between Versace and Chanel."

"Played my biggest ever gig tonight. Sell-out crowd, four encores."

Sei Shonagon, a Japanese woman who lived 10,000 years ago, wrote a diary full of gossip, advice, jokes and lists of likes and dislikes.

The artist Frida Kahlo included sketches and paintings in her diary.

"Good day today. Rescued a planeload of people, foiled a bank robbery, saved the world. Took afternoon off."

Pssst... Use your diary to analyse things that bother you and think of solutions. Avoid being unkind about other people.

Samuel Pepys, who wrote a detailed diary in the 1660s, described important events such as wars, plagues and the Great Fire of London.

Private ~keep out!

Your diary is personal and not for sharing – which is why nosy brothers or sisters would love to get hold of it! Avoid this by writing your diary in private and keeping it somewhere safe. Here are some more top-secret tips.

Sneaky spots

Think carefully about where to hide your diary. Don't go for obvious places such as under the bed or in a drawer. If your diary is small and slim, make this crafty pocket.

1. Wrap a large rectangle of **felt** over your diary.

2. Stitch the sides so the diary can slip in and out easily.

3. Tape your secret pocket to the back of a picture or wall mirror…

… or sew it on to a coat hanger, then cover it with clothes.

Fold the top flap over the hanger and stitch in place.

Clever camouflage

Think smart and disguise your diary as an exercise book so dull that nobody will give it a second look. Stack it casually with school books and you can be sure it will never be read!

Which would you be most tempted to open? This…

MATHS JOTTER

…or this?

PRIVATE DO NOT READ!

Codes and symbols

Writing in code protects private information, but it takes time, so you may not want to do it every day. Many codes substitute letters of the alphabet for a symbol or another letter.

Dictionary codes

Grab a big dictionary (with more than a thousand pages) and try this brilliant code – it's fiendishly tricky to crack and doesn't use a written **key** that someone could find.

Ancient Egyptians used pictures to mean certain things. You could try this too.

1. *Look up the word you want and write down the page number. Make the number four digits long by adding zeros in front if necessary.*

2. *Now write 1 or 2, depending on whether the word is in the first or second column, then count down the entries in that column and write the position of your word. If it's a single digit, add a zero in front.*

disaster

(first column, second entry)

368
(page number)

0368102

3. *Do the same for each word to make a series of 7-digit numbers, meaningless to everyone… except you.*

0368102 – 0780212
0879122 1005209!

(Disaster – lost my phone!)

Pssst… *If you don't mention that you keep a diary, then no one will go looking for it.*

Fantastic photos

Photos are often the best kind of keepsake. They bring back great memories instantly, perhaps of important days, fabulous holidays, or people you love. Displaying photos stops them getting crumpled or lost, and means you can admire them whenever you want.

Photo albums

One obvious place to put photos is in an album. Choose one with large, self-adhesive pages so you can arrange your photos freely and stick them in place easily. You could also buy **corner mounts** and stick photos into scrapbooks.

Think smart

Albums are expensive and soon fill up! Squeeze in extra photos by overlapping them on the page, making sure you don't cover important bits.

Clever cuts

Another way of saving space is to crop photos – in other words, cut out sections you don't need. Don't slice off too much or you won't be able to tell where the photo was taken.

Pssst... Try cutting around people or objects to create unusual photo shapes.

Fab frames

A frame is a great way of displaying a favourite photo, either hanging on the wall or standing on your desk or bedside table. Choose a style and colour of frame that suits your image, or decorate a plain wooden frame with glued-on buttons or shells.

You can also frame certificates, posters or even T-shirts.

The first proper photograph was taken in 1826 in France. The photographer had to leave the camera for eight hours to take the picture!

Hand-held cameras became popular around 1900, and were bulky and box-shaped.

Photo facts

Digital photo frames store hundreds of images and scroll through them as a slideshow.

Scrapbook basics

Pssst... Why not put together a scrapbook as a thoughtful gift for someone special?

To make photo albums more interesting, why not add tickets, letters and other souvenirs to create a scrapbook? If you don't fancy filling a whole book, design individual pages to frame or keep in a ring binder. Here's what you need to start scrapbooking.

School Trip to Paris: Day 1

Plan each page

Before you stick anything down, plan your scrapbook carefully. Each page needs a theme, so give it a title, then decide what to include. Choose a mix of photos and other mementoes.

Don't cram in too much – if you have several similar photos, pick just one.

Remember that you can crop photos (see page 17) to save space.

Now plan your layout. Start with one large, important element, then position everything else around it. To make things stand out more, try mounting them on card in a **contrasting** colour and overlapping them at a slight angle.

Glue things in place when you're happy with the design, then add captions, labels or notes.

School Trip to Paris: Day 1

This is from the bonbons Ethan (!) gave me.

Our waiter looked a bit like this!!

Emily checks the map yet again...

Now turn the page for more advanced scrapbooking ideas and techniques!

Stylish scrapping

There are many clever ways of making scrapbooks look really professional. Here are a few to try – but don't use them all at once, or your pages will be too fussy!

Glam it up

Small decorations, called **embellishments**, are useful for filling gaps and adding extra dazzle. You can buy these from craft shops but the cost soon adds up, so try making your own. For example, tie a bow in a scrap of lace or ribbon, cut paper flowers or sprinkle on glitter.

Rough and smooth

Create interesting texture combinations by layering thick, grainy paper on shiny gift wrap, or tear paper rather than cutting it to leave arty, rough edges.

Torn strips of paper make great borders for scrapbook pages.

Rip it up

Here's another effective torn paper technique. Fold a piece of paper in half and draw a shape next to the fold.

Tear around the line, then open out the finished shape. Use the torn shape to mount a photo and the rest of the paper to frame another.

Have fun!

Scrapbooks are often filled with memories that make you smile, so have some fun with your layouts. A Halloween page might have googly eyes dotted over a black background and silly ghost jokes under flaps. You could also give photos funny captions or even turn a sequence of photos into a comic strip.

Finishing touches

Don't spoil a great design with messy, smudged handwriting! Choose good-quality pens and write slowly and neatly, or make letters with stencils instead. Use a computer to create titles and captions in all kinds of fancy **fonts**.

Pssst… Give photos extra impact by sticking small squares of foam or cardboard on the back to raise them off the page.

Creative displays

Filling your room with favourite photos and mementoes is a great chance to use your imagination and have some fun. Here are some brilliantly easy ideas for really inventive displays.

Arty arrangements

If you have space, put photos in several similar-coloured frames and arrange them on the wall in a neat interlocking design. If you prefer something less precise, tack up snap after snap until you've covered the wall in one enormous **photomontage**!

Pretty pegs

If you're short of wall space, why not clip photos, cards and other keepsakes on pegs? Use plain wooden or plastic clothes pegs and paint or decorate them however you want. String up a length of wool, ribbon or fairy lights and hang the pegs from it.

How about taking one big picture and framing it in sections, like this?

Covered cork boards

Cork boards are handy for displaying paper mementoes – but the pins leave holes in your stuff. Avoid this by making a stylish cork board cover with fabric and ribbon.

1. *Put the cork board inside a pillowcase and push it to one corner.*

Choose a colour or pattern that matches your room decor.

2. *Fold the edges of the pillowcase over the back of the board and stick them down with strong tape. Stretch the fabric tightly.*

3. *Cut a length of ribbon long enough to cross the board diagonally and fix it in place with drawing pins at the back.*

4. *Fix more lengths of ribbon across the board, then repeat in the other direction to make a diamond pattern. Press a drawing pin into each ribbon cross.*

5. *Slide photos, tickets, letters, postcards and other bits and bobs under the ribbon.*

Pin a loop of ribbon at the back to hang your board.

Pssst... Ask an adult for help when hanging frames or cork boards.

Storage solutions

Keepsakes are often treasured collections. You can collect anything – dolls, soft toys, figurines, key rings, buttons, tickets, badges, erasers... you name it! Whatever your collection, it needs to be stored safely and arranged attractively.

Only collect things you love – don't copy your friends.

Hooks are ideal for bags, skates and other mementoes that can be hung up.

On display

Shelves, bookcases and windowsills are obvious places to display candles, money boxes and other large objects, while glass cabinets stop things getting too dusty.

Cool containers

Small items such as beads, coins or stickers may be best kept in boxes, jars or tins. Charity shops are brilliant places to find unusual and attractive containers, while clear plastic boxes are useful if you want to see what's inside.

Handy pockets

To store bits and bobs, make felt pockets like the one on page 14 and decorate them. Cover a cork board with fabric (see page 23) and pin your pockets to it.

Use cheerful, bright thread.

Sew on beads, buttons, felt shapes or bows.

Decorated tins

Give a biscuit tin a stylish new look by covering it with glossy pictures. This is called **découpage**. Choose images that suit your theme – for example, sea creatures to cover a tin of shells.

1. Cut lots of images from magazines. Mix some PVA glue with a little water, so it's runny.

2. Spread glue over the lid and sides, then cover with pictures, brushing each with glue as you stick it down. Leave to dry.

Overlap pictures and don't leave gaps.

Pssst... For a glossy finish, paint on a layer of clear nail varnish – but do it near an open window as the fumes are strong!

Crazy collections

Some people have huge collections of objects such as spoons, crisp packets, tea bags and traffic cones!

A special 'gnome reserve' in Devon displays the world's biggest gnome collection – 2,042 in total.

Stamp collecting is one of the most popular hobbies ever. In 2011, one rare stamp sold for more than £1,000,000.

Think practical

There's a limit to how many keepsakes you can display before your room becomes cluttered! Give some precious mementoes a practical purpose so they're useful rather than gathering dust.

Why not fill a clay pot with pencils? Or recycle that souvenir boomerang into a coat hanger?

Photos galore

It's easy and fairly cheap to have photos printed on all kinds of things including key rings, clothes, mouse mats, phone covers, bags, calendars and more. Look for photo services in large supermarkets or online.

Get photos of friends printed on mugs, so you can see them whenever you have a drink!

Brilliant bookmarks

Tickets are the perfect shape for bookmarks. Mount them on card first so they last longer.

Make more bookmarks by cutting greetings cards, postcards, photos or maps into strips and mounting them on card. Add decorations such as ribbon, then carefully stick wide, clear tape over the bookmark to protect it.

T-shirt cushions

Don't fill drawers with old T-shirts too special to throw out – transform them into cute cushions instead! All you need is a needle, thread and a soft filling, such as old towels, socks, jumpers or pillow stuffing.

Use thread the same colour as the T-shirt so it doesn't show.

1. Turn the T-shirt inside out. Carefully sew up the arm holes, then along the bottom. Use small, neat stitches to nip the material together.

2. Turn the T-shirt the right way and stuff it, pushing material right into the corners.

3. Seal up the neck hole by stitching the **seams** together.

More clothes cushions

Other kinds of clothes make funky cushions, too – how about experimenting with shorts or skirts? Turn vest tops inside out, sew straight across the top, then stuff and sew up in the same way as a sleeved T-shirt.

Pssst... A T-shirt cushion makes a clever hiding place for a finished diary. Push your diary deep inside the stuffing before stitching up the neck.

Making memories

Looking back over old diaries and precious keepsakes is great fun – so the more you have, the better! Here are some hints and tips to help you keep creating fantastic memories.

Start snapping!

It's easy to take photos with a camera phone, so take a few pictures whenever you're having a good time. But make sure you upload them on to a computer or print copies in case you accidentally delete them.

Get sorted

You must be organized to create good albums, scrapbooks and displays. Keep photos and other memorabilia in order and write the date, place and useful information on the back. These details may seem obvious now, but in a few years' time you'll have forgotten completely!

End of term picnic, 29 May 2013, Castledene Park.

Left to right:
Sam, me, Jo, Ellie, Sophie.

Pssst... The sooner you put photos and mementoes into albums or scrapbooks, the more detail you'll remember, and the more enthusiastic you'll be to include it all.

Go out and about

If you want photos of fab parties, make sure you're invited to a few! The more friendly and outgoing you are, the more fun you can have with others. Why not join after-school clubs or plan weekend trips with friends?

Keep writing

Stay in touch with far-off friends or cousins by email, then print their replies and keep any letters and cards. You could also ask friends to send you funny postcards whenever they go on holiday!

Take photos of your family on special occasions or days out.

Start a **family tree** and hunt for fascinating old photos.

Glossary

acid-free
Without the natural acids that make materials gradually discolour and fall apart over time.

blog
Short for 'web log'; an online diary that often allows readers to add comments to entries.

contrasting
Something very different. Putting two contrasting colours together can help make each stand out.

corner mounts
A small, self-adhesive photo corner. Slip one on each corner of your photo before sticking them in place on the page.

découpage
The technique of decorating a surface with paper cut outs.

diarist
Someone who writes a diary, especially one which is then published.

embellishment
An extra detail or decoration added to make something look more interesting or beautiful.

family tree
A diagram showing information about members of a family and how they are related.

felt
Fabric made from matted wool. Felt is easy to cut, cheap to buy and comes in lots of different colours.

font
A style of lettering. If you're using a very decorative font on the computer, make sure it can be read clearly.

heirloom
Something that has been in a family for years, passed from one generation to the next.

key
A list of meanings of coded letters or symbols, or a clue to work them out.

photomontage
The technique of making a collage from photos.

PVA glue
A strong, water-based glue, also known as white craft glue.

quotation
A few words or a longer piece of writing, perhaps from a book or speech, that you want to remember. Good quotations are funny, wise or meaningful to you in some way.

review
A report on something (such as a book, play, TV programme, film or music), describing whether you think it is good or bad and explaining why.

seam
A line or ridge where two pieces of fabric have been sewn together.

treasury tag
A short string with a metal bar at each end, used to hold papers together.

Smart sites

www.ehow.com/how_2161152_write-a-diary.html
Essential diary-writing tips, help and advice.

www.artistshelpingchildren.org/journalsdiariescraftskidshowtomakediary.html
Arty ideas for inventive and unusual diary covers and decorations.

www.wikihow.com/Create-Secret-Codes-and-Ciphers
How to create fantastic codes to use in a top-secret diary.

http://tlc.howstuffworks.com/family/picture-frames.htm
Lots of imaginative picture frame designs using all kinds of materials.

www.spoonful.com/create/scrapbooking-ideas-keepsakes-gallery
Fantastic scrapbooking ideas plus creative ways of displaying keepsakes.

http://tlc.howstuffworks.com/family/paper-desk-organizers.htm
Easy ideas for making desk organizers for your bedroom.

Index